ABOUT THIS STUDY:

You feel like you're in over your head. The challenge feels like it's beyond you. Or maybe you are in an unfamiliar place. Or both. Bottom line... this reality is absolutely not your comfort zone. Maybe you feel ready to dive in. Maybe you're a little nervous... or a lot nervous.

Timothy was there. Paul had given him an enormous responsibility, one that moved him from understudy to the lead role in a fledgling church. Overwhelmed is probably an understatement. Guided by the Spirit, Paul wrote Timothy a letter that spoke to him in that moment. Imagine Timothy opening this letter and hearing both Paul and the Holy Spirit speak calming words and pointed advice that flowed out of a very profound, yet simple focal point.

Love. Pursue it and everything else will fall in line. It's simple, but not easy. It depends on the power and grace of the Creator. It must come from pure and unmixed motives, a conscience focused on good and right things and a genuine faith in a living and active God that has a plan and a purpose for His people. Timothy needed that letter. This week, so do you.

LOVE...

1 TIM 1:3-7

I0164609

ontrack devotions
EXPEDITION

www.OnTrackDevotions.com

OnTrack Expedition: Love: 1 Timothy 1:3-7

Printed in the United States of America

Copyright © 2015 Pilgrimage Educational Resources

Author: Dennis M. Wilhite
Executive Developer: Benjamin J. Wilhite
Graphic design by Lance Young (higherrockcreative.com)

ISBN-13 978-0692479162
ISBN 0692479163

10 9 8 7 6 5 4 3 2 1

1 TIM 1:3-7 (ESV)

The end purpose of your assignment is...

LOVE

Out of:

...a pure heart

...a good conscience

...and genuine faith

3 As I urged you when I was going to Macedonia, remain at Ephesus so that you may charge certain persons not to teach any different doctrine, 4 nor to devote themselves to myths and endless genealogies, which promote speculations rather than the stewardship from God that is by faith. 5 The aim of our charge is love that issues from a pure heart and a good conscience and a sincere faith. 6 Certain persons, by swerving from these, have wandered away into vain discussion, 7 desiring to be teachers of the law, without understanding either what they are saying or the things about which they make confident assertions.

PASSAGE
INTRO NOTES

Record key ideas from the passage introduction or from your first read through the entire passage. Write down any "big questions" on the tag below so you can revisit them during the week.

o†d
EXPEDITION

BIG questions this week...

1: SET GOALS

This exercise is designed to help prepare your heart and mind for the week of your upcoming event. Take some time to get alone and answer them. Good goals should be specific and measurable.

(1) Complete the following sentences to help you formulate some goals for the week:

This week, I hope I...

This week, I hope we as a group...

(2) Complete the following sentences to help you begin to formulate a strategy for seeing the above goals fulfilled:

In light of my answers above, I must...

In light of my answers above, we must...

EXPEDITION

(3) Complete the following sentences to help you formulate a plan to avoid what will derail your goals:

In light of my answers, I must not...

In light of my answers, we must not...

2: PLAN & COMMIT

Take your responses from the previous questions and write out a "personal commitment" for the week. That is, what are you going to personally commit to be doing this week and commit to not be doing. You will sign it and seek out at least one other person on the trip who will read it, pray for its fulfillment, and keep you accountable to it. If possible, seek out a second witness that will not be part of the event group that will pray for you during the event and will check in with you afterward to see how it went.

I, _____, personally commit to

I further commit to not

Name: _____

Signature: _____

Witness#1: _____

Witness#2: _____

Date: ___/___/___

1ST DAY ASSIGNMENT

1: JOURNAL

Experiences
What experiences have you faced in the last 24 hours?

Questions
What questions do you find yourself asking?

Conclusions
What kind of conclusions are you coming to about yourself and others?

OCD EXPEDITION

2: READ 1 TIMOTHY
Read the entire book through like you would read a letter. Pay special attention to the particulars of what Timothy's responsibilities are.

3: EVALUATE
Answer the questions below based on today's reading.

What was Timothy's assignment? What challenges were involved?

How do you think Timothy reacted to the assignment? Are there any hints in the letter?

What is your assignment this week as it relates to your role in the group? What is your assignment back home?

How are you doing in fulfilling that assignment? Why? Identify external challenges and internal obstacles standing in the way this week and at home.

What do you need to do in order to better fulfill your assignment? Here? At home?

4: INTEGRATE
Spend some time on each of the following activities to get the most out of today's study.

Memorize 1 Cor 13:1-3

Pray
Spend some time praying for yourself and for others in your group.

Commit
In light of what you see in yourself so far, what personal commitment will you make for today? Write it down...

Today, I'm praying for...

I commit to...

2ND DAY
PURPOSE

1: JOURNAL

Experiences
What experiences have you faced in the last 24 hours?

Questions
What questions do you find yourself asking?

Conclusions
What kind of conclusions are you coming to about yourself and others?

O⳨d
EXPEDITION

2: READ 1 TIMOTHY
Reread the entire book. Pay special attention to the particulars of the end purpose behind Timothy's assignment.

3: EVALUATE
Answer the questions below based on today's reading.

Based on Paul's letter to Timothy what does love look like?

What is the relationship between love (the goal) and the assignment (the task)?

How does seeing love as the goal change how you understand your assignment this week? At home?

How selflessly are you pursuing the best interest of others this week? At home?

What inside of you stands in the way of such absolute love?

4: INTEGRATE
Spend some time on each of the following activities to get the most out of today's study.

Memorize 1 Cor 13:1-3

Pray
Spend some time praying for yourself and for others in your group.

Commit
In light of what you see in yourself so far, what personal commitment will you make for today? Write it down...

Today, I'm praying for...

I commit to...

1: JOURNAL

Experiences
What experiences have you faced in the last 24 hours?

Questions
What questions do you find yourself asking?

Conclusions
What kind of conclusions are you coming to about yourself and others?

2: READ 1 TIMOTHY
Reread the entire book. Watch for what a pure heart looks like.

OⓉD EXPEDITION

3: EVALUATE
Answer the questions below based on today's reading.

What does the text indicate might be characteristics of a heart (motivation) that is pure (unmixed)?

How does a pure heart make absolute love possible?

Where does a pure heart come from?

What would single-hearted love look like in the carrying out of your assignment this week? At home?

How single-hearted are your motivations this week? At home? What motivations compete with your call to love?

4: INTEGRATE
Spend some time on each of the following activities to get the most out of today's study.

Memorize 1 Cor 13:1-3

Pray
Spend some time praying for yourself and for others in your group.

Commit
In light of what you see in yourself so far, what personal commitment will you make for today? Write it down...

Today, I'm praying for...

I commit to...

1: JOURNAL

Experiences
What experiences have you faced in the last 24 hours?

Questions
What questions do you find yourself asking?

Conclusions
What kind of conclusions are you coming to about yourself and others?

2: READ 1 TIMOTHY
Reread the entire book looking for what a good conscience looks like.

3: EVALUATE
Answer the questions below based on today's reading.

What does the book indicate might be characteristics of a good conscience? Is a good conscience one that works well or is one that is clean?

Where do you think a good conscience comes from?

Why does a good conscience make absolute love possible?

What would a good conscience look like in your challenges and experiences this week? At home?

How well is your conscience functioning? What are the indicators?

4: INTEGRATE
Spend some time on each of the following activities to get the most out of today's study.

Memorize 1 Cor 13:1-3

Pray
Spend some time praying for yourself and for others in your group.

Commit
In light of what you see in yourself so far, what personal commitment will you make for today? Write it down...

Today, I'm praying for...

I commit to...

5TH DAY
GENUINE FAITH

1: JOURNAL

Experiences
What experiences have you faced in the last 24 hours?

Questions
What questions do you find yourself asking?

Conclusions
What kind of conclusions are you coming to about yourself and others?

2: READ 1 TIMOTHY
Reread the entire book looking for what a good conscience looks like.

OGD
EXPEDITION

3: EVALUATE

Answer the questions below based on today's reading.

How does the text describe genuine faith? How does that contrast with a show faith?

How does genuine faith make absolute love possible?

How would you know if you have genuine faith by looking at how you carry out your assignment this week? At home?

What are the doubts that compromise your leadership this week? At home?

What needs to happen to increase your faith?

4: INTEGRATE

Spend some time on each of the following activities to get the most out of today's study.

Memorize 1 Cor 13:1-3

Pray
Spend some time praying for yourself and for others in your group.

Commit
In light of what you see in yourself so far, what personal commitment will you make for today? Write it down...

Today, I'm praying for...

I commit to...

1: EVALUATE

This exercise is designed to help discover and record the key takeaways from the week. Take some time to work through the process so you will get the most out of it.

(1) Take some time to read back through the pre trip contract you signed at the beginning of the week.

Write down some of the occasions where you fulfilled your commitment this week.

Write down some of the occasions where you struggled with your commitment this week.

List some of the experiences God used this week to challenge you in light of your commitment.

(2) Read back through your daily journal entries and Bible study notes and answer the questions below.

In what ways did you assignment (experience) this week take you out of your comfort zone? In what ways did it compare and contrast with your "real life" back home?

How loving do you think you were this week to those around you? Was it easier or harder than loving people in your "real life" back home? Why do you think that is?

Based on your experience and responses this week, how pure do you think your heart is? What do you think your primary challenges are to purifying your heart as you transition back to "real life?"

How did your conscience (good or bad) impact your capacity to fulfill your assignment this week? What will it take to both protect and purify your conscience as you transition home?

How was your faith challenged and/or grown this week? Is your faith more genuine now than it was at the beginning of the week?

What did your experience this week reveal to you about your relationship to God and how it affects the love you have to give to others?

2: APPLY

This exercise is designed to help connect your key takeaways to "real life" at home. Take some time to work through each of the steps below.

(1) Take a minute and think about what things will be like when you get home. Write down your thoughts.

What are you most looking forward to?

What are you least looking forward to?

(2) Where do you think it'll be most difficult to live out what you've learned?

(3) Where do you think it will be easiest to live out what you've learned?

OCD
EXPEDITION

3: COMMIT

Take your responses from the previous questions and write out a "personal commitment" for your transition to "real life." That is, what are you going to personally commit to be doing and commit to not be doing at home. You will sign it and seek out at least one other person from the trip who will read it, pray for its fulfillment, and keep you accountable to it. Also seek out a key person at home to share your commitment(s) with that will encourage you, pray for you and hold you accountable.

I, _____, personally commit to

I further commit to not

Name: _____

Signature: _____

Witness#1: _____

Witness#2: _____

Date: ___/___/___

MEET THE AUTHOR

Dr. Dennis Wilhite began his career as an educator in 1991 after 20 years of local church ministry. He currently teaches a range of student ministry, discipleship, and leadership courses for Summit University (PA). He also instructs graduate courses for Liberty Baptist Theological Seminary's online program and is an academic mentor for other distance program professors.

Dr. Wilhite served as the student ministries pastor, then interim senior pastor at First Baptist Church (North Tonawanda, NY) from 1971 to 1980, then accepted the call to fill the student ministries position at Calvary Baptist Church (Grand Rapids, MI) where he served until 1990. His focus has been discipling people for the work of the ministry both in his years in the local church and in his ministry at Summit University.

In 1972, Dr. Wilhite took his first wilderness trip as a youth pastor. Twelve years later, he launched Pilgrimage to help grow other ministry leaders in their capacity to leverage the wilderness environment for ministry outcomes. Over a quarter century later, Pilgrimage is a leading provider of ministry wilderness programming, including the addition of accredited college and graduate courses through several Christian colleges and universities.

Dennis Wilhite, EdD

Role: Professor

Where: Summit University (PA)

Family: Married w/4 children and 8 grandchildren

Online:
SimplyAPilgrim.com
SummitU.edu

EDITION

o❈d
ontrack devotions

WANT TO GROW SELF-FEEDERS?

EQUIP THEM... WITH A DEVOTIONAL TOOL THAT WORKS.

ONTRACK IS A DEVOTIONAL TOOL DESIGNED TO BUILD THE SKILL AND DISCIPLINE OF EFFECTIVE DAILY BIBLE STUDY FOR STUDENTS AND ADULTS. ITS UNIQUE APPROACH MODELS INDUCTIVE BIBLE STUDY METHODS AND ADDS VALUE FOR SMALL GROUP ACCOUNTABILITY THROUGH MONTHLY COMMITMENTS. OTD WALKS THE USER THROUGH A PROCESS OF DISCOVERY, UNLOCKING THE WORD BY TRAINING THEM HOW TO ASK GOOD QUESTIONS THROUGH REPETITION AND MODELING. TIME IN THE WORD BECOMES A REAL CONVERSATION WITH GOD. AVAILABLE IN DIGITAL AND PRINT EDITIONS.

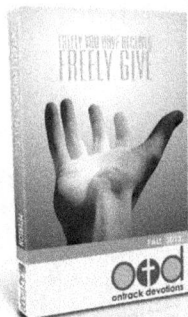

PRINT EDITION
*3 SEASONAL VOLUMES PER YEAR
*PACES WITH MINISTRY SEASONS
*AS LOW AS $1.67 PER PERSON/MO

DIGITAL EDITION

DIGITAL EDITION
*MONTHLY PDF DOWNLOADS
*PRINTABLE IN BOOKLET FORM
*LICENSE FOR ENTIRE CHURCH LOCATION
*AS LOW AS $20.75/MO
(ANNUAL SUBSCRIPTION)

WHAT MINISTRY LEADERS ARE SAYING...

WE'RE BIG FANS OF ONTRACK DEVOTIONS. IT'S SOLID, RELEVANT CONTENT THAT CHALLENGES TEENAGERS TO EMBRACE THE LIFE OF A CHRIST-FOLLOWER.

LES BRADFORD
YM360.COM

THERE IS NOTHING QUITE LIKE IT. I USE OTD DAILY AND WE USE IT IN OUR MINISTRIES SUCH AS URBAN HOPE (INNER CITY MINISTRY) AND MOMENTUM (YOUTH CONFERENCE).

ED LEWIS
BUILDMOMENTUM.ORG

PILGRIMAGE

PILGRIMAGE EDUCATIONAL RESOURCES / CLARKS SUMMIT, PA
P: 570.504.1463 / E: INFO@SIMPLYAPILGRIM.COM / SIMPLYAPILGRIM.COM

THE ONTRACK DEVOTIONS MILITARY EDITION IS A 12-MONTH STUDY THROUGH THE NEW TESTAMENT AND PROVERBS WRITTEN FOR TODAY'S MILITARY PERSONNEL. THE INCLUDED USER GUIDE WALKS THE READER THROUGH THE BASIC STEPS OF INDUCTIVE BIBLE STUDY (OBSERVATION, INTERPRETATION, APPLICATION, IMPLEMENTATION), ALLOWING THEM TO START AT THEIR CURRENT SKILL LEVEL AND DIVE INTO THE MEAT OF THE WORD OF GOD.

WHETHER YOU ARE A CHAPLAIN LOOKING FOR RESOURCES FOR YOUR UNIT, A CHURCH WITH ACTIVE DUTY MEMBERS OR A SOLDIER, SAILOR, AIRMAN OR MARINE THAT NEEDS A FIELD-READY DEVOTIONAL GUIDE, MOTD FITS THE BILL. THE YEAR IS BROKEN DOWN INTO 12 ONE-MONTH SECTIONS WITH A USER GUIDE THAT INTRODUCES THE "WHY" AND "HOW" OF INDUCTIVE BIBLE STUDY.

FOLLOW AND LIKE MILITARY DEVOS FOR DAILY DEVO THOUGHTS:

@MILITARYDEVOS
FACEBOOK.COM/MILITARYDEVOS

MILITARYDEVOTIONAL.COM

PILGRIMAGE EDUCATIONAL RESOURCES
1362 FORDS POND RD
CLARKS SUMMIT, PA 18411

www.ingramcontent.com/pod-product-compliance
Lightning Source LLC
Chambersburg PA
CBHW060550030426
42337CB00021B/4526